1

Mind Power

> See to it that no one takes you captive through philosophy and empty deception, according to the tradition of men, according to the elementary principles of the world rather than according to Christ.
>
> Colossians 2:8

> When the Son of Man comes, will He find the faith on the earth?
>
> Luke 18:8

Christianity may well be facing the greatest challenge in its history: a powerful and growing seduction that is subtly changing biblical interpretations and undermining the faith of millions of people. Most Christians are scarcely aware of what is happening, and much less do they understand the issues involved.

The seduction is surprisingly easy. It does not take place as an obvious frontal assault from rival religious beliefs. That would be vigorously resisted. Instead, it comes to some Christians in the guise of faith-producing techniques for gaining spiritual power and experiencing miracles and to others as self-improvement psychologies that are seen as scientific aids to successful Christian living. Or it may take other forms. Charles Colson has written:

> I have spoken of the frontal assaults and the sneak attacks. There is something worse. . . . The enemy is in our midst. He has so infiltrated our camp that many simply no longer can tell an enemy from a friend, truth from heresy.[1]

A Trojan Horse Inside the Church?

Even the leading cult-watchers have generally failed to recognize the Trojan horse that has penetrated both the church and their own ranks and is seducing from within.

The bait on the pagan hook has always been the promise of godhood that the Serpent offered to Eve. The attempt to realize this godhood has involved the human race in numerous forms of occultism throughout its history. One word that is often used to encompass all occult practices is "sorcery." In the following pages, when we use that word our intended meaning will be: any attempt to manipulate reality (internal, external, past, present, or future) by various mind-over-matter techniques.

THE NEGATIVE SIDE OF POSITIVE THINKING

Dave Hunt
T.A. McMahon

HARVEST HOUSE PUBLISHERS
Eugene, Oregon 97402

Except where otherwise indicated, all Scripture quotations in this book are taken from The New American Standard Bible, Copyright © 1960, 1962, 1963, 1968, 1971, 1972, 1973, 1975, 1977 by the Lockman Foundation. Used by permission.

Verses marked KJV are taken from the King James Version of the Bible.

THE NEGATIVE SIDE OF POSITIVE THINKING

Taken from **THE SEDUCTION OF CHRISTIANITY**
Copyright © 1985 by Harvest House Publishers
Eugene, Oregon 97402

ISBN 0-89081-683-2

All rights reserved. No portion of this book may be reproduced in any form without the written permission of the Publisher.

Printed in the United States of America.

Contents

1. Mind Power 5
   A Trojan Horse Inside the Church?
   Sorcery: The Unrecognized Enemy
   Success Is the Name of the Game
   Think and Grow Rich
   The "Supreme Secret": A Counterfeit Faith
   Contending for the Faith

2. Supplication or Spiritual Law? 19
   Mind Science: Linking Christianity
      and Sorcery
   Is God a Placebo?
   Inside Dealing
   The Real Issue

3. From Words to Images 29
   New Thought: The New Revival
   The Power of "Self-Talk"
   The New "Science of the Mind"
   Imagination and Human Potential
   Fact or Figment?
   From Words to Images
   How to Meet Your Own Jesus?
   The Danger of the Mental Picture
   Idolatry and Demons
   Summary

Strangely enough, most of today's Christian leaders who rightly cry so mightily against so many evils are saying little if anything about the revival of *sorcery* that is sweeping both the secular world and the church. In many cases it reflects a lack of awareness or naiveté, and in some cases an unwillingness to admit their own involvement. Why is this? It is because most Christians are so uninformed about occultism that they wouldn't recognize it except in its most blatant forms. Nor do very many Christians seem to understand the passages in the Bible forbidding occult practices, so they cannot recognize sorcery on that basis either. The extent to which anti-Christian and even occult beliefs and methodologies have been integrated into Christianity within the last few years is staggering, and this trend is now accelerating at an alarming rate.

Sorcery: The Unrecognized Enemy

What the secular world calls "mind power" many Christians confuse for "faith." Likewise, the impersonal "Force" that occultists also refer to as Universal Mind or Nature is naively accepted by large numbers of both Christians and non-Christians as just another way of referring to God, when in fact it is a substitute for Him. Consequently, what often passes for "the power of the Spirit" in the church can scarcely be distinguished from the alleged "mind powers" of psychics. Parapsychologists have been conducting scientific experiments with psychics for years, and the idea of "psychic power" is gaining credibility.

Professional psychics are no longer as unique as they were only a few years ago, but now number in the hundreds and are being taken seriously by a large segment of society. Moreover, similar "mind powers" are being developed by the general populace through a smorgasbord of psychological methodologies. These are not only taught by well-known mind-over-matter cults such as Scientology, the Forum (formerly est— Erhard Seminars Training), Lifespring, and the Silva Method (formerly Silva Mind Control), but are the standard fare at today's PMA (Positive Mental Attitude) motivational and success seminars. The ability to exert "Mind over matter" is no longer considered to be something weird or occult, but is now thought to be part of a natural, normal, yet *infinite* human potential that can be experienced by anyone who follows certain alleged "laws of success."

Many modern practitioners, including leading Christians, seem unaware of the true nature of the dangerous mind-game they are playing. Sorcery called by any other name is still sorcery, and it is everywhere in today's space-age society, seeking to hide its true identity behind psychological terminology and success/motivation and self-development labels.

An occultist himself and one of the world's leading occult authorities and historians, Manly P. Hall has declared:

> . . . there is abundant evidence that in many forms of modern thought—

especially the so-called "prosperity" psychology, "will-power building" metaphysics and systems of "high-pressure" salesmanship—black magic has merely passed through a metamorphosis, and although its name may be changed, its nature remains the same.[2]

Success Is the Name of the Game

Success is the name of the game today, not only out there in the world, but inside the church as well. Humility is out and self-esteem is in, even though we are urged in Scripture, "Let each esteem others better than themselves" (Philippians 2:3 KJV). It used to be common knowledge that the besetting sin of the human race was pride. Now, however, we are being told that our problem is not that we think too highly of ourselves, but too lowly, that we all have a bad self-image, and that our greatest need is to build up our self-esteem. Though Peter wrote, "Humble yourselves, therefore, under the mighty hand of God, that He may exalt you at the proper time" (1 Peter 5:6), we are being urged to "visualize" ourselves into success. Paul's inspired declaration that Christ "emptied Himself, taking the form of a bond-servant . . . [and] humbled Himself by becoming obedient to . . . death on a cross" (Philippians 2:7,8) is now explained by Robert Schuller, in the context of today's success-oriented world, to mean:

> Jesus knew his worth, his success fed his self-esteem. . . . He suffered the cross to sanctify his self-esteem. And he bore the cross to sanctify your self-esteem.
>
> And *the cross will sanctify the ego trip* [emphasis in the original]![3]

As Christianity's "number one TV preacher,"[4] Robert Schuller is watched on nearly 200 TV stations each Sunday by an audience of nearly 3 million.[5] According to *Christianity Today*, "Schuller is now reaching more non-Christians than any other religious leader in America."[6] Schuller's influence is enormous, and his "Gospel of Success"[7] is being accepted and preached by increasing numbers of Christian leaders. What does Schuller find wrong with the old gospel? Although Paul wrote that "Christ Jesus came into the world to save sinners" (1 Timothy 1:15), and Christ Himself said that He came to call "sinners to repentance" (Luke 5:32), Robert Schuller writes:

> I don't think anything has been done in the name of Christ and under the banner of Christianity that has proven more destructive to human personality and, hence, counterproductive to the evangelism enterprise than the often crude, uncouth, and unchristian strategy of attempting to make people aware of their lost and sinful condition.[8]

especially the so-called "prosperity" psychology, "will-power building" metaphysics and systems of "high-pressure" salesmanship—black magic has merely passed through a metamorphosis, and although its name may be changed, its nature remains the same.[2]

Success Is the Name of the Game

Success is the name of the game today, not only out there in the world, but inside the church as well. Humility is out and self-esteem is in, even though we are urged in Scripture, "Let each esteem others better than themselves" (Philippians 2:3 KJV). It used to be common knowledge that the besetting sin of the human race was pride. Now, however, we are being told that our problem is not that we think too highly of ourselves, but too lowly, that we all have a bad self-image, and that our greatest need is to build up our self-esteem. Though Peter wrote, "Humble yourselves, therefore, under the mighty hand of God, that He may exalt you at the proper time" (1 Peter 5:6), we are being urged to "visualize" ourselves into success. Paul's inspired declaration that Christ "emptied Himself, taking the form of a bond-servant . . . [and] humbled Himself by becoming obedient to . . . death on a cross" (Philippians 2:7,8) is now explained by Robert Schuller, in the context of today's success-oriented world, to mean:

> Jesus knew his worth, his success fed his self-esteem. . . . He suffered the cross to sanctify his self-esteem. And he bore the cross to sanctify your self-esteem.
>
> And *the cross will sanctify the ego trip* [emphasis in the original]![3]

As Christianity's "number one TV preacher,"[4] Robert Schuller is watched on nearly 200 TV stations each Sunday by an audience of nearly 3 million.[5] According to *Christianity Today*, "Schuller is now reaching more non-Christians than any other religious leader in America."[6] Schuller's influence is enormous, and his "Gospel of Success"[7] is being accepted and preached by increasing numbers of Christian leaders. What does Schuller find wrong with the old gospel? Although Paul wrote that "Christ Jesus came into the world to save sinners" (1 Timothy 1:15), and Christ Himself said that He came to call "sinners to repentance" (Luke 5:32), Robert Schuller writes:

> I don't think anything has been done in the name of Christ and under the banner of Christianity that has proven more destructive to human personality and, hence, counterproductive to the evangelism enterprise than the often crude, uncouth, and unchristian strategy of attempting to make people aware of their lost and sinful condition.[8]

It used to be said, "All who desire to live godly in Christ Jesus will be persecuted" (2 Timothy 3:12), but today it is said, "Those who live godly lives will be honored and in this world will achieve success." Not just individual Christians, but churches also now pursue success, and the larger the church the more successful it is considered to be. On that basis, by far the most successful pastor in the world is Paul Yonggi Cho, who heads the world's largest church, with about 400,000 members. Cho teaches that positive thinking, positive speaking, and positive visualizing are the keys to success.

Christian colleges, seminaries, missions, and relief organizations are also in the success game, and most of them look to the techniques of big business for running their own affairs. If it works for the University of California, why not for a Christian college? If it works for General Motors, why not for a Christian relief organization? This is no doubt true when it comes to certain things such as accounting and management. However, sorcery is rampant in the business world and enters the church in the form of success/motivation and PMA techniques and the latest psychotherapies baptized with Christian terminology.

Think and Grow Rich

Most of the masters of business success/motivation and PMA techniques have been seduced into sorcery, and are seducing millions of other people as well. Most of the basic ideas and techniques behind self-improvement courses that literally permeate society today can be traced back to one man, Napoleon Hill.

Hill's best-selling book *Think and Grow Rich* is listed by top motivational speaker Og Mandino as one of the twelve greatest self-help books of all time.[9] Napoleon Hill's books are offered at Christian bookstores across the country and are recommended by numerous Christian leaders even though these books contain some of the most blatant occult teachings one could find anywhere. If Christians who recommend his writings offer a word of caution, they do so only concerning Hill's emphasis upon wealth. Yet it is Hill's teachings *about the mind* that are far more dangerous than his emphasis on wealth. Hill explains in some detail that he learned the mind-power techniques contained in his books from disembodied spirit entities:

> Now and again I have had evidence that unseen friends hover about me, unknowable to the ordinary senses. In my studies I discovered there is a group of strange beings who maintain a school of wisdom. . . .
>
> The School has Masters who can disembody themselves and travel instantly to any place they choose . . . to give knowledge directly, by voice. . . .
>
> Now I knew that one of these Masters had come across thousands of miles, through the night, into my study. . . .

"You have earned the right to reveal a Supreme Secret to others," said the vibrant voice. "You have been under the guidance of the Great School. . . . Now you must give the world a blueprint. . . ."[10]

The "Supreme Secret": A Counterfeit Faith

The secrets of success that form the foundation for most success/motivation books and seminars were given to Hill by demons posing as "Masters who can disembody themselves and travel instantly to any place they choose." The "Supreme Secret" they authorized Hill to "reveal" to the world has been preserved in occult tradition for thousands of years and reminds one of the Serpent's offer of godhood to Eve: *"Anything the human mind can believe, the human mind can achieve"* [emphasis in the original].[11] If it is indeed true that we can achieve *anything* we conceive, then we must be gods. This "secret of the ages" is also called by Hill "The Magic Power of Belief."[12] Its basic premise is that the human mind has mysterious, inherent powers that are capable of creating one's own reality: "Truly, deeply believe you will have great wealth, and you will have it."[13] This is the sorcerer's counterfeit "faith" and is the basis for what the secular world calls PMA (Positive Mental Attitude). The "PMA Science of Success"[14] was made famous by Napoleon Hill in *Success Through A Positive Mental Attitude*, which he co-authored with

W. Clement Stone as a guide for tapping into "the great universal storehouse of Infinite Intelligence, wherein is stored all knowledge and all facts, and which may be contacted through the subconscious. . . ."[15]

Far from having the gracious and loving, but sovereign, God as its object of trust, this "power of belief" enables those who have been initiated into its secrets to *command* forces to obey their thoughts. If *anyone* can "make a miracle happen," then it isn't a genuine miracle from God, but sorcery, and man is now playing God.

Nor is it only the liberals who are falling into this trap. Presbyterian pastor Ben Patterson of Irvine, California, has observed:

> Of late, evangelicals have out-liberaled the liberals, with self-help books, positive-thinking preaching, and success gospels.[16]

Anyone who imagines that because he thinks certain thoughts or speaks certain words God *must* respond in a certain way, has slipped into sorcery, and, if not playing God, is at the very least attempting to manipulate God. Charles Capps, one of the leaders in the Positive Confession Movement, says, "This is not theory. It is fact. It is spiritual law. It works every time it is applied correctly. . . . You set them [spiritual laws] in motion by the words of your mouth . . . everything you say—will come to pass."[17]

Yonggi Cho declares:

> By the spoken word we create our universe of circumstances. . . .[18]

> You create the presence of Jesus
> with your mouth. . . . He is bound
> by your lips and by your words. . . .[19]

The similarities between what these Christian leaders teach and the "Supreme Secret" given to Hill by demonic beings to share with the world is at the least highly disturbing. We are not condemning everything else a Christian leader writes or speaks simply because he quotes Napoleon Hill. Yet it is because Hill is mixed in with so much good that his concepts are accepted. This is why we must be on our guard and contend for the purity of the Word of God without addition of deadly deceptions that creep in unawares.

Contending for the Faith

Jude wrote that we must "contend earnestly for the faith which was once for all delivered to the saints" (Jude 3). It is impossible to always be "positive" while contending for truth. H. A. Ironside, longtime pastor of Moody Memorial Church in Chicago, declared: "The faith means the whole body of revealed truth, and to contend for all of God's truth necessitates some negative teaching. . . . Any error, or any truth-and-error mixture, calls for definite exposure and repudiation. To condone such is to be unfaithful to God and His Word, and treacherous to imperiled souls for whom Christ died."[20] Dave Wilkerson, a pastor, best-selling author, and founder of Teen Challenge, has said:

Let it be known once and for all, God will not abdicate His lordship to the power of our minds, negative or positive. We are to seek only the mind of Christ, and His mind is not materialistic; it is not focused on success or wealth. Christ's mind is focused only on the glory of God and obedience to His Word.

No other teaching so ignores the Cross and the corruption of the human mind. It bypasses the evil of our ruined Adam nature, and it takes the Christian's eye off Christ's gospel of eternal redemption and focuses it on earthly gain.

Saints of God, flee from this! . . .[21]

2
Supplication or Spiritual Law?

> O God, the nations [pagans] have invaded Thine inheritance.... Help us, O God of our salvation.
> Psalm 79:1,9

Mind Science: Linking Christianity and Sorcery

Ernest Holmes founded the Church of Religious Science, also known as Science of the Mind, upon the "Supreme Secret" that the "Masters of Wisdom" revealed to Napoleon Hill. It is closely related to the positive thinking of Norman Vincent Peale and the possibility thinking of Robert Schuller. (In fact, Peale credits Holmes with making him into a positive thinker.[1]) Here is the way Holmes explained this "Supreme Secret":

> SCIENCE OF MIND teaches that
> Man controls the course of his life . . .

by mental processes which function according to a Universal Law . . . that we are all creating our own day-to-day experiences . . . by the form and procession of our thoughts.[2]

Man, by thinking, can bring into his experience whatsoever he desires . . . [emphasis in original].[3]

This idea has taken firm hold in our modern world. It has become the major link between sorcery and Christianity. Though expressed in slightly different phrases, it is the common language of all those who have, wittingly or unwittingly, replaced faith in God with a self-serving faith in some mysterious Force that can be used by our minds to get what we want. Norman Vincent Peale is, of course, one of the most successful evangelists of the power of the mind. He explains it like this:

Your unconscious mind . . . [has a] power that turns wishes into realities when the wishes are strong enough.[4]

Is God a Placebo?

Robert Schuller's *possibility thinking* is the same product as Peale's *positive thinking* marketed under a different brand name. Schuller declares: "Now—Believe and You Will Achieve."[5] Paul Meyer, the president of Success Motivation Institute, expresses it this way: "Vividly imagine, sincerely believe, ardently desire, enthusiastically act and it must inevitably come to pass."[6]

Paul Yonggi Cho declares: "Through visualization and dreaming you can incubate your future and hatch the results."[7] Such teaching has confused sincere Christians into imagining that "faith" is a force that makes things happen because they *believe*. Thus faith is not placed *in* God but is a power directed *at* God, which forces Him to do for us what we have *believed* He will do. When Jesus said on several occasions, "Your faith has saved [healed] you," He did not mean that there is some magic power triggered by believing, but that faith had opened the door for Him to heal them. If a person is healed *merely because he believes he will be healed*, then the power is in his mind and God is merely a placebo to activate his belief. If everything works according to the "laws of success," then God is irrelevant and grace obsolete.

In contrast to the biblical doctrine of grace, this insistence that God Himself must work even His own miracles within a framework of laws that enables us to tap into and dispense spiritual power by what we think, speak, or do is the basis for ritualism and occultism.

Inside Dealing

In sorcery everything works by established esoteric formulas. When the witch doctor slits the rooster's throat, sprinkles the blood in a certain pattern, and chants a formula, the gods *must* come through because they are bound by "spiritual laws" to do so. By his knowledge of the spiritual laws, the priest (whether wizard, medicine man, or witch doctor) has become the special intermediary between the people and the gods. The arrangement between the priest and the spirit world is called the "magician's bargain." What seems to the awestruck people to be a "miracle" is actually the result of this "inside deal," which is believed to be produced by the spiritual laws that govern not only the occultist but the spirits as well (who sell power for human souls).

The Bible forbids humans to attempt any contact or bargain with the spirit world (Deuteronomy 18:9-14). It can only lead to disaster, even though at first there may seem to be genuine healings and feelings of love and peace. There is no cause-and-effect relationship between man and spirits, whether angels or demons, any more than between man and God, yet evil spirits encourage this idea in order to deceive and enslave. We must never forget that our *only* approach to God is as unworthy sinners relying upon His grace and love. Although they may not intend it, the Positive Confession teachers often present in a biblical framework occult theory and methodologies that lead to delusion. The biblical teaching of *supplication* has been replaced by the idea that we can get God to do whatever we want to by following the rules of the game. In reference to a house she wanted to buy, Gloria Copeland relates:

> I began to see that I already had authority over that house and authority

over the money I needed to purchase it. I said, "In the Name of Jesus, I take authority over the money I need. (I called out the specific amount.) I command you to come to me . . . in Jesus' Name. Ministering spirits, you go and cause it to come."

(Speaking of angels . . . when you become the voice of God in the earth by putting His Words in your mouth, you put your angels to work! They are highly trained and capable helpers; they know how to get the job done.)[8]

We do not believe the leaders of the Positive Confession Movement are deliberately involved in sorcery. However, the terminology, while sounding biblical, promotes concepts that cannot be found in the Bible, but are found in occult literature and practice. Moreover, some of the Positive Confession leaders not only admit but teach that the methods, laws, and principles they use are also used successfully by occultists. Nowhere in the Bible does it indicate or even imply that the people of God are to use the same methods or power as the pagans. Yonggi Cho, however, not only says that miracles must all conform to what he calls the "Law of the Fourth Dimension,"[9] but that *anyone*, including occultists, can "apply the law of the fourth dimension and . . . perform miracles."[10]

It sounds like the "dark and light sides of the Force." Nevertheless, pastor Cho assures us that he learned this from "the Holy Spirit" when he asked in prayer why occultists could do miracles just like Christians.[11] Cho commends the Japanese Buddhist occultists, the Soka Gakkai, for performing "miracles" through visualizing "a picture of prosperity, repeating phrases over and over [and] . . . develop[ing] the human spiritual fourth dimension."[12] And he scolds Christians for not doing likewise.[13] *Prophecy & Economics Newsletter* publisher Frank Goines states that anyone, Christian or not, can—

> . . . totally control his own flow of God's riches [because there] is a law of Prosperity . . . [that] can be used by *anyone*. . . .
>
> Prayer is a scientific application following an exact law [emphasis in the original].[14]

The Real Issue

If *everything* is part of a cause-and-effect process governed by physical or spiritual laws, then it follows that: 1) anyone or anything, including God or gods, must be part of this process and bound by these laws; 2) there is no act of creation out of nothing and thus no Creator separate and distinct from His creation; 3) there can be no supernatural, for *everything* (including the actions of the gods) would be governed by *natural* laws; and 4) godlike powers are available to anyone.

On the other hand, if creation was not the result of a *natural* process governed by *natural* laws, then it must have been a *supernatural* event requiring a Creator. This fact forces us to the following conclusions: 1) since the very origin of the universe is a miracle, it is clear that miracles can repeatedly occur; 2) if miracles are to occur, they can only result from the *independent action of the Creator*; and 3) since miracles by very definition are not governed by laws of any kind, there is no ritual, formula, prayer, or demand that anyone can use to bring about a miracle; it must be by grace alone. We can rely upon God's *promises* because of His integrity and love—not because He is bound by "scientific law."

The Creator God of the Bible is not subject to such laws, nor is He in a cause-and-effect relationship with His creation, or else He would be part of a problem to which there would be no real solution. Because He is outside of nature, God is not affected by the disease, decay, and death that now exist and are bringing inevitable destruction upon the entire universe. Indeed, the cosmos has the stamp of death upon it because it is separated from its Creator by the rebellion of Satan and of man and is therefore under God's judgment: "The wages of sin is death."

But the transcendent God of the Bible can reach in from outside, effecting His miracles. These include the whole range of triumph over natural law; but the most important miracles are forgiveness of sin, redemption, resurrection, and the creation of new creatures for a new universe that He will someday bring into existence for the redeemed to inhabit. Having given us the power of choice so that we could freely choose to respond to His love, He will not violate our wills. And unlike the bargaining and appeasing involved with pagan gods, our approach to the God of the Bible must be as unworthy sinners relying upon His grace and mercy, recognizing that there are no formulas that we can think or speak that will require Him to respond to us in a certain way.

We must come to God on His terms, believing that through the virgin birth He became a man to die for our sins, and that having paid the penalty we could never pay, He rose from the dead and is now alive, seeking an entrance into the hearts of all who will receive Him as Savior and Lord. To admit that the true God is not bound by laws opens the door to miracles and closes the door on occultism and ritual magic, which are man's attempt to play God. In doing this man no longer has *control* of himself or the universe. That is the issue.

3
From Words to Images

> To obey [God] is better than sacrifice. . . . Rebellion is as the sin of divination [witchcraft], and insubordination is as iniquity and idolatry.
> 1 Samuel 15:22,23

> Therefore, my beloved, flee from idolatry. . . . The things which the Gentiles sacrifice, they sacrifice to demons, and not to God.
> 1 Corinthians 10:14,20

Sorcery promises power to heal and transform through contact with a parallel universe of the spirit, from which this mysterious energy is allegedly drawn. That contact is said to be made in our minds: The thoughts we think and the words we speak become the vehicles of spiritual power. Those who accept this concept become victims of the great delusion that displaces God with self. In seeking power for self, they have become susceptible to the power of Satan. Nevertheless, even as the irrefutable evidence mounts documenting its destructive and evil power, sorcery's popularity and general acceptance is exploding in the secular world and, in "Christianized" forms, is gaining increasing acceptance within the church.

Even among evangelicals, we are seeing an astonishing acceptance of heresies that are reminiscent of the radical teaching of the Transcendentalists (Ralph Waldo Emerson, Henry Thoreau, William Channing, Bronson Alcott, et. al.), who introduced an intellectualized form of sorcery into America in the early nineteenth century. The Transcendentalists sparked a successful revolt against then-dominant New England Fundamentalism. Similar teaching is being revived today, but this time Fundamentalism itself is being revolutionized from the inside.

New Thought: The New Revival

Transcendentalism helped spawn what became known as New Thought, which emphasized that *thought* controls everything. Forced out of the church at that time as heresy, New Thought became the basis for such mind-science cults as Christian Science, Religious Science, and Unity. Today's church is being swept by a revival of New Thought (now called Positive Thinking, Possibility Thinking, Positive Confession, Positive Mental Attitude, and Inner Healing). We are very concerned that this time New Thought, which represents inside the church what New Age is in the secular world, will not be forced out, but will remain within the evangelical church.

At Unity headquarters near Kansas City, Missouri, Dr. Robert Schuller addressed a large audience of Unity ministers and ministers-in-training, sharing with them how his ministry had grown and showing them how they could apply the same principles to improve the growth of Unity. Asked to describe the role of what he might consider a New Age minister in the 1980s, Schuller made no protest that he knew nothing of the New Age or that he wasn't a "New Age minister." Without hesitating, he replied:

> Well, I think it depends upon where you're working. I believe that the responsibility in this Age is to "positivize" religion. Now this probably doesn't have much bearing to you people. Being Unity people, you're positive. But I talk a great deal to groups that are not positive . . . even to what we would call Fundamentalists who deal constantly with words like sin, salvation, repentance, guilt, that sort of thing.
>
> So when I'm dealing with these people . . . what we have to do is positivize the words that have classically only had a negative interpretation.[1]

The Power of "Self-Talk"

One method advocated for reinforcing positive affirmations is called "self-talk." This idea was pioneered by Emile Coue in the early 1900s. His magic phrase "Every day and in every way I am becoming better and better" swept Europe and America, healed organic diseases, and transformed lives before falling into disrepute.[2] Under different labels this idea is being revived again, and Christian psychology has brought it into the church. Although he tries to differentiate his brand of "self-talk" from Positive Confession, pastor and clinical psychologist David Stoop states:

> The power released by our Self-Talk is incredible. Not only do our thoughts and words create our emotions, they have the power to make us well or sick, and to determine our future.
>
> This renewed emphasis on the power of the mind reflects a swing back to ancient ideas concerning the interrelationship of the body and the mind. . . .
>
> These principles are universal. . . . Think you're getting a cold? Watch out, you've got it! . . . Think your kids are going to act up at Grandma's house? Never fails.[3]

Here not only psychosomatic symptoms are alleged to be produced by what one thinks, but even the behavior of the "kids at Grandma's"!

Such ideas used to be termed superstition, but are now deemed scientific because they have become incorporated within psychology's conflicting mind/spirit theories and therapies. Agnes Sanford writes: ". . . a vibration of very, very high intensity and an extremely fine wave-length, with tremendous healing power, caused by spiritual forces operating through the mind of man, is the next thing science expects to discover."[4] Such ideas, once the dream of the ancient alchemists, are today the Holy Grail of psychology. Although they are no nearer to finding it and no more scientific than their predecessors, many Christian psychologists hold out this "carrot on the stick" to anguished souls seeking a peace and joy that earlier Christians found in the crucified and risen Christ alone. Denis Waitley counsels:

> Perhaps the most important key to the permanent enhancement of self-esteem is the practice of positive self-talk. Every waking moment we must feed our self-images positive thoughts about ourselves and our performances, so relentlessly and vividly that our self-images are in time molded and modified to conform to new, higher standards.[5]

The New "Science of the Mind"

Biblical truth is no longer the solution, but flattery and fantasies of the mind. What used to be called pride is now called "positive self-talk," and is as diligently cultivated today as it was formerly struggled against. The almost canonical authority given to psychology within the church makes what would otherwise be obviously erroneous seem sensible to Christians and even scientific. In another of his books hailed by top Christian leaders, Waitley suggests that "positive self-talk" be recorded and listened to repeatedly to improve "health, self-esteem, and creative growth."[6] The seductive manner in which sorcery is deliberately masqueraded as "science" in order to give it wide acceptance can be understood from the following statement in *New Thought* magazine:

> Something wonderful has been happening behind the scenes in both science and non-denominational worship . . . researchers are able to show that we ARE spiritual beings, creatures of light and cosmic substance, and that our lives are the product of our thinking apparatus and how we use that computer-like device to create holograms of our "reality". . . .
>
> The growing demand for self-help products indicates that the time has come for this information to be a basic topic from kindergarten upward. But, unless we name it something else—like "bioenergetic physics"—it's going to remain a religious idea and subsequently stay out of our schools. . . .

> This should not be blacked out of
> our schools. This is not religion. This
> is a science. In the final analysis, per-
> haps it is the only science there is.[7]

Under the guise of science, basic sorcery has been introduced into public schools. The church has also fallen for the same delusion. Lutheran pastor Bill Vaswig declares: "Agnes Sanford has believed in God's 'light' in terms of real energy for many years. In many ways her belief has been sustained by modern physics and psychology."[8] As an example of how this works, Vaswig writes: "We visualized the light and energy of God entering the woman's body and healing her completely. We held her up in our imaginations . . . [and] thanked God that it was so."[9]

Imagination and Human Potential

In the world of success/motivation seminars, imagination is considered to be the key that unlocks infinite human potential—and this is passed off as the latest scientific discovery coming out of the new physics. Waitley suggests that "positive self-talk" should not be listened to consciously, but that the "right-brain" should be allowed to "record" it in the unconscious as "images and feelings about yourself. . . ." He adds emphatically: *"Who you see in your imagination will always rule your world."*[10] This is no suggestion that we focus our attention upon our Lord. Instead of "being transformed into Christ's image" through meditating upon His glory by faith (2 Corinthians 3:18), we are being taught to visualize ourselves as we want to be in order to transform ourselves into the likeness of this fantasy image. Waitley declares: "As you see yourself in the heart of your thought, in your mind's eye, so you do become."[11] Pastor and author C. S. Lovett states:

> Imagination is the key to creation. Everything God is doing He first sees in His mind. And so it is with men made in His image. . . .
> While our faith allows us to accept what we can't see . . . imagination takes us a step beyond, allowing us to PICTURE what we cannot see. Isn't that remarkable! [emphasis in the original.][12]

Fact or Figment?

The mental images that one is able to *picture* or visualize are no longer looked upon as mere figments of the mind, but as reality *created* by the mind that can even impact the physical world. The metaphysical philosophy underlying Positive Thinking and Possibility Thinking as well as major aspects of the Positive Confession Movement is founded upon the alleged power inherent within thoughts and words. Charles Capps says, *"Words are the most powerful thing in the universe."*[13] God presumably used this power residing within words to create the universe, and that same power is allegedly available to us as creatures *"in God's class very capable of operating in the same kind of faith."*[14] How does this work? Capps explains:

> Words are containers. They carry faith, or fear, and they produce after their kind. . . . God is a faith God. God released His faith in Words [emphasis in original].[15]

In the occult, thoughts, words, and mental images have the same power as idols and are closely linked. New Thought brought this concept into Christianity, which is where Agnes Sanford picked it up, and this is the source of the prayer techniques that she taught to so many who are now leaders in the church. In his definitive work, *Hindu Polytheism*, Alain Danielou states: "To the original or true language belong the sacred utterances used in worship and called *mantras*. The word *mantra* means 'thought-form' "[16] The Hindu scriptures declare: ". . . they go to Hell who think that the image is merely a stone and that the Mantra is merely a letter of the alphabet. All letters [words] are forms of Shakti [force] as sound-powers."[17] There are numerous cults in America today that represent attempts to syncretize Hindu mantra power with New Thought and pseudo-Christianity. The Church Universal and Triumphant headed by Elizabeth Clare Prophet (Guru Ma) is one of the best known. Prophet declares:

> With the science of the spoken Word . . . incisive invocations in the form

of decrees to the ascended Masters help in solving specific problems. . . .

Since the essence of prana does extend and permeate all of Matter . . . by the spoken Word we can also send it out into a world in need of healing. So sound is the great command.[18]

The Bible does not teach such methods. Their danger lies in the fact that these mind techniques produce mental states that become a substitute for the real solution, which the Christian is to find through his relationship with Christ in the walk of faith.

From Words to Images

The most powerful way that occultists use thoughts is to visualize some particular "thought-form" in the mind. This methodology has been adopted by Humanistic and Transpersonal psychologies; and under the umbrella of Christian psychology has come into the church. Dardik and Waitley state: "Visualization works because the mind reacts automatically to the information we feed it in the form of words, pictures and emotions. . . . The act of vividly imagining a scene in your mind makes it a real experience."[19] Originator of Silva Mind Control Jose Silva agrees: "If you operate according to some very simple laws, the imaginary event will become real. . . . The better you learn to visualize, the more powerful will be your experience with Mind Control."[20]

Occultists have long held that through visualization, thoughts can be materialized into existence on the physical plane. In their book *Thought-Forms*, Annie Besant and C. W. Leadbeater declare that "the creation of an object is the passing out of an image from the mind and its subsequent materialization . . . [which] becomes for the time a kind of living creature . . . [called] 'an elemental.' "[21]

Visualization brings surprisingly easy contact with what witch doctors and other shamans have always called "spirits." Anthropologist Michael Harner, in his book, *The Way of the Shaman*, explains that "the shaman has at least one, and usually more, 'spirits' in his personal service. . . ."[22] Modern man follows the same shamanistic procedures and contacts the same "spirits" but calls them "inner guides" or "imaginary guides."

In visualizing "God" or "Jesus," the average Christian is not aware that he is following the same procedure that shamans insist opens a "magic doorway" in the mind that leads to the sorcerer's world. This simple but powerful technique has long been used by shamans for entering the spirit realm in order to contact and bargain with spirit entities. It is also being promoted and taught by an alarming and increasing number of Christian leaders, who urge us to visualize our concept of "Jesus" and promise that the image we create in our minds will become the *real* Jesus, who will then make genuine contact with us.

How to Meet Your Own Jesus?

Those pursuing healing and success often fall

prey to the temptation to accept whatever seems to work, and to adjust their interpretation of the Bible accordingly. Christians are being taught to "visualize" themselves on a beautiful, sandy beach or a peaceful, grassy knoll, and to "see" Jesus approaching them. All over America, specialists in healing of the memories are leading entire congregations to visualize Jesus as present at some traumatic childhood or even prenatal event, which He sanctifies, forgives, or changes—and in the process delivers them from their past.

There may indeed be something in the past that must be dealt with which is causing bitterness against those who may have wronged us and whom we have never forgiven, or guilt for things we have done to others and never apologized for or made right. No Christian should continue for one more moment with anything like that on his conscience, and need not. All that we need for dealing with such problems is found in the fact that Christ died for our sins and has risen from the dead to live His life in us. No one who has truly received God's love and forgiveness as a sinful rebel can possibly withhold that same love and forgiveness from those who have wronged him. We love and forgive others because of God's love and forgiveness to us. It is that simple. This is the "fruit of the Spirit" that results from Christ living in us.

Jesus carefully told His disciples that He was going away, and that He would send the Holy Spirit to be with them. The Comforter has come, and we know His presence in our lives by faith in His promise and by the experience of the fruit of the Spirit. *Visualization* of God or Jesus plays no part in this, is not necessary, and is in fact an attempt to make Him *appear* rather than to know His abiding presence. Our Lord certainly gave no instruction nor even hinted that anyone should *visualize* Him and that He would then appear.

The New Testament records a number of appearances of Jesus to His disciples during the 40 days after His resurrection and prior to His ascension, and even afterward to Paul on the Damascus road. Never is there a hint that any of these appearances were initiated by anyone except the Lord Himself, much less that they were brought about by visualization.

There is a genuine contact with Christ through faith, a communion in the heart that He gives to His own. He may even appear as He wills for some specific purpose. But to create a fantasy Jesus in our minds and insist that this is the *real* Jesus and that talking with this figment of our imagination is the way to genuine spiritual experience is to be deluded indeed. It is only marginally different, but still a delusion, to attempt to create an atmosphere of high suggestibility that will enable us to "feel" His presence or somehow encourage Him to appear. In any such techniques, the definite possibility exists of opening the door to demonic contact, while acquiring an "inner guide" that we think is the real Jesus.

The Danger of the Mental Picture

The danger of the mental picture is that it

seems to be real. For some, the experience validates itself and transcends any objective evaluation, even the Bible. But we do well to heed the words of J. I. Packer:

> . . . we take the second commandment—as in fact it has always been taken—as pointing us to the principle that (to quote Charles Hodge) "idolatry consists not only in the worship of false gods, but also in the worship of the true God by images."
>
> In its Christian application, this means that we are not to make use of visual or pictorial representations of the Triune God, or of any person of the Trinity, for the purposes of Christian worship. . . .
>
> . . . it is certain that if you habitually focus your thoughts on an image or picture of the One to whom you are going to pray, you will come to think of Him, and pray to Him, as the image represents Him. Thus you will in this sense "bow down" and "worship" your image; and to the extent to which the image fails to tell the truth about God, to that extent you will fail to worship God in truth. That is why God forbids you and me to make use of images and pictures in our worship. . . .
>
> To follow the imagination of one's heart in the realm of theology is the

way to remain ignorant of God, and to become an idol-worshiper—the idol in this case being a false mental image of God, "made unto thee" by speculation and imagination.[23]

Idolatry and Demons

Paul gives a powerful reason against idolatry when he explains that in worshiping idols the Gentiles are really worshiping devils: "No; but I say that the things which the Gentiles sacrifice, they sacrifice to demons, and not to God; and I do not want you to become sharers in demons" (1 Corinthians 10:20). Scripture makes it clear that we can only know the true God as He really is, and that we must come to Him on His terms. Satan or demons, however, will hide behind any mask and answer to any image or name. They are very broad-minded in their various ruses to get humans under their power.

Paul seems to be saying that not just *some* idols but *all* idols are fronts for demons. This is what makes visualization of Jesus or God not just a minor error but extremely dangerous. That visualization is ideally suited for contact with demons can be demonstrated in the fact that it has been used for that very purpose for thousands of years in various forms of sorcery. And the sorcerer will always tell you that it doesn't matter what image you conjure up, but conjure up an image you must.

Summary

It should be clear by now that using visualization techniques to change traumatic or unpleasant events in our lives is a Christianized form of the mental alchemy that attempts to manipulate reality. At the very least this unscriptural practice denies God's omnipotence by implying that He needs our "creative visualization" to apply effectively His forgiveness and healing; and at worst, it sets us up as gods who can, through prescribed rituals, use Him and His power as our tools.

We are not chained to the past until visualization therapy in some form sets us free. We are free in Christ. He is our life. That life does not need any unbiblical therapy. We become born again the day He comes into our hearts.

Since that day the Holy Spirit works in the life of every child of God, transforming his heart and mind. What counts is our love for Him, our simple faith in His Word, and our obedience to the leading of His Spirit in the present.

NOTES

CHAPTER ONE

1. Charles Colson, *The Struggle For Men's Hearts and Minds* (Prison Fellowship, 1983), p. 16.
2. Manly P. Hall, *Masonic, Hermetic, Qabbalistic and Rosicrucian Symbolical Philosophy* (Los Angeles, 1969, Sixteenth Edition), pp. CI, CII.
3. Robert Schuller, *Living Positively One Day at a Time* (Revell, 1981), p. 201; and *Self-Esteem, The New Reformation* (Word Books, 1982), p. 115.
4. *Eternity*, Nov. 1983, Lloyd Billingsley, "The Gospel According to Schuller," p. 23.
5. *Time*, Mar. 18, 1985, p. 70; *Los Angeles Times*, May 29, 1983, p. 1.
6. *Christianity Today*, August 10, 1984, pp. 23-24.
7. Ibid.
8. *Christianity Today*, Oct. 5, 1984, p. 12.
9. Og Mandino, *The Greatest Secret in the World*, p. 276.
10. Napoleon Hill, *Grow Rich With Peace of Mind* (Ballantine Books, 1967), pp. 158-60.
11. Ibid., p. 176.
12. Ibid.
13. Ibid.
14. Napoleon Hill and W. Clement Stone, *Success Through A Positive Mental Attitude* (Pocket Books, 1977), p. 55.
15. Ibid., p. 72.
16. *Christianity Today*, Mar. 1, 1985, "Is God a Psychotherapist?" by Ben Patterson, pp. 22-23.
17. Charles Capps, *The Tongue—A Creative Force* (Harrison House, 1976), pp. 24, 131, 132.
18. Paul Yonggi Cho, *Solving Life's Problems* (Logos, 1980), p. 51.
19. Paul Yonggi Cho, *The Fourth Dimension* (Logos, 1979), p. 83.
20. H.A. Ironside, "Exposing Error: Is It Worth While?" Tract.
21. David Wilkerson, "A Prophecy Wall of Fire," available from World Challenge, Inc., P.O. Box 260, Lindale, TX 75771.

CHAPTER TWO

1. James Reid, *Ernest Holmes: The First Religious Scientist* (Science of Mind Publications, Los Angeles), p. 14.
2. "The Viewpoint in the Science of Mind Concerning Certain Traditional Beliefs" (Science of Mind Publications).
3. Ernest Holmes, *The Science of Mind* (textbook), p. 30, cited in *Science of Mind*, September 1983, p. 47.
4. Norman Vincent Peale, *Positive Imaging* (Fawcett Crest, 1982), p. 77.
5. Robert Schuller, *Tough Times Never Last, But Tough People Do* (Bantam Books, 1984), p. 161.
6. Mack R. Douglas, *Success Can Be Yours* (Zondervan, 1977), p. 37.
7. Cho, *Fourth*, op. cit., p. 44.
8. Gloria Copeland, *God's Will Is Prosperity* (Harrison House, 1978), pp. 48-49.
9. Cho, *Fourth*, op. cit. p. 50.
10. Ibid., p. 64.
11. Ibid, pp. 36-43.
12. Ibid., p. 64.
13. Ibid.
14. Frank Goines, *Best of Prophecy & Economics Newsletter*, p. 53.

CHAPTER THREE

1. Robert Schuller, address at Unity Village, Unity tape.
2. Dave Hunt, *Peace, Prosperity, and the Coming Holocaust* (Harvest House, 1983), pp. 117-20.
3. David Stoop, *Self-Talk: Key to Personal Growth* (Revell, 1982), p. 135.
4. Agnes Sanford, *The Healing Light* (Macalester, 1947), p. 32.
5. Denis Waitley, *The Winner's Edge*, p. 80.
6. Denis Waitley, *Seeds of Greatness*, pp. 60-61.
7. *New Thought*, Autumn 1983, Ann B. Martin, "The Great American Educational Blackout," p. 6.

8. William L. Vaswig, *I Prayed, He Answered* (Augsburg, 1977), pp. 55-56.
9. Ibid., pp. 51-52.
10. Waitley, *Seeds*, p. 61.
11. Waitley, *Winner's*, p. 61.
12. C.S. Lovett, *Longing To Be Loved* (Personal Christianity, 1982), p. 85.
13. Capps, *Tongue*, p. 129.
14. Ibid., p. 130.
15. Ibid., pp. 132, 135.
16. Alain Danielou, *Hindu Polytheism* (Pantheon Books), p. 28.
17. Sir John Woodroffe, *The Garland of Letters: Studies in the Mantra-Shastra*, (Ganesh & Co.), p. 261.
18. *The Coming Revolution*, Spring 1981, Elizabeth Clare Prophet, "The Control of the Human Aura Through the Service of the Spoken Word," p. 36.
19. Irving Dardik and Denis Waitley, *Quantum Fitness*, p. 37.
20. Jose Silva and Philip Miele, *The Silva Mind Control Method* (Pocket Books, 1977), pp. 32, 36.
21. Annie Besant and C.W. Leadbeater, *Thought Forms* (The Theosophical Publishing House, 1971), pp. 3, 15.
22. Michael Harner, *The Way of the Shaman* (Harper & Row, 1980), p. 20.
23. J.I. Packer, *Knowing God* (Inter-Varsity Press, 1973), pp. 40-42.

Harvest Pocket Books

These compact pocket books are excerpted from bestselling, full-length Harvest House books. Each booklet gives the major thrust of the complete book in an inexpensive, condensed version, designed for readers on the go. Further material on each topic can be obtained by purchasing the full-length edition.

Falling in Love Again — ISBN 6212
David and Carole Hocking (from *Good Marriages Take Time*)

Bedroom Talk — ISBN 6220
David and Carole Hocking (from *Good Marriages Take Time*)

Making Your Time Count — ISBN 6794
Emilie Barnes (from *More Hours in My Day*)

Overcoming Temptation—Don Baker — ISBN 6808
(from *Lord, I've Got a Problem*)

Your Will, God's Will — ISBN 6816
Lloyd John Ogilvie (from *Discovering God's Will in Your Life*)

Understanding the New Age Movement — ISBN 6824
Dave Hunt (from *Peace, Prosperity and the Coming Holocaust*)

The Negative Side of Positive Thinking — ISBN 6832
Dave Hunt and T.A. McMahon (from *The Seduction of Christianity*)

Surviving Divorce—Jim Smoke — ISBN 6840
(from *Growing Through Divorce*)

When You Feel Hurt—Dwight Carlson — ISBN 6859
(from *Overcoming Hurts and Anger*)

How to Beat the Blahs—Florence Littauer — ISBN 6867
(from *Blow Away the Black Clouds*)

Healthy Sexuality — ISBN 6875
Joseph and Mary Ann Mayo (from *What It Means To Be a Woman*)

Understanding Your Child's Behavior — ISBN 6883
Beverly LaHaye (from *How to Develop Your Child's Temperament*)

This booklet has been excerpted from Dave Hunt and T.A. McMahon's 550,000-copy bestseller— an accurate look at the health, prosperity, and success movement in the church:

The Seduction of Christianity

Bestselling authors Dave Hunt and T.A. McMahon examine the dangerous doctrines and practices influencing millions through Christian television, religious books, and Christian magazines. The apostle Paul wrote of a "deluding influence" that would come upon the world in the last days leading to widespread apostasy. The same spirit of deception that is rampant in the secular world is now influencing the church. Christians need to become aware of these unbiblical doctrines so they won't fall prey to the *Seduction of Christianity*.

*Available at
Christian bookstores everywhere*

DAVE HUNT has become internationally known for such significant bestselling books as *The Seduction of Christianity, Beyond Seduction, The Cult Explosion,* and *America: The Sorcerer's New Apprentice*. A recognized cult expert, his research and consulting expertise takes him around the world.

T.A. McMahon holds a master's degree in communications and has researched and written numerous Christian documentaries.